The Daily Haiku Reader

The Daily Haiku Reader

Everyday Mindfulness Through the Seasons

The Playhard Press

Asheville Bellingham Ithaca

dailyhaiku.app
playhardpress.com
playhardproject.com

ISBN 978-1-954305-16-8

Dedication

For Jun Noguchi, sleeping on the beach
Maritza Ljungström, traveling under the stars
and The Bowery Poetry Club, where poets come to dream

Introduction

There are moments in our lives that stay with us ever after. The way a leaf in autumn lingers, slowly slipping to the ground, or how the full-moon reflects off the water on a still summer night—these intimate moments of connection bring us closer to knowing ourselves and the world around us. They make us mindful of the present moment and bring awareness to our lives. Sharing such experiences is the very heart of haiku.

Readers might identify a *haiku* as a seventeen-syllable poem with lines of five, seven, and five syllables. Although commonly accepted, this simple definition omits the nuance and subtlety for which this writing tradition is revered. Capturing and conveying the essence of a stirring moment is the true challenge, not counting syllables. After all, Japanese poets compose in *logographic characters*—they do not actually count syllables at all. Rather, they listen for *onji,* or the "sound symbols" in Japanese phonetic script. One syllable in English may have two or more onji by Japanese standards. Nevertheless, the concept of a five, seven, five syllable meter persists as a reasonable approximation for haiku written in English and other Roman alphabet languages.

As the Japanese language evolved, it came to be spoken in twelve short sounds at a time, usually with a break after the fifth and seventh sounds. By the 10th century, poets were imitating this natural rhythm by composing short poems called *tanka*. These tanka were written with major rhythmical breaks after five, seven, and five sounds, followed by two lines of seven sounds. These classical era poets would meet to share their tanka, with carefully measured onji. By the 13th century, serious tanka poets were showing their poetic prowess at elite social gatherings. Several poets would collaborate and write a long poem, called a *renga*. Each poet added a stanza of seventeen sounds in lines of five, seven, and five. This created a long chain of collaborative tanka they would deliver to an eager crowd. Modern haiku was born from the humble opening stanza of a renga, called the *hokku*, which had the important function of setting the season for the piece.

These poets adhered to rules that were part of the game, established by centuries of precedent. Having the correct flow of onji to create a pleasant rhythm was essential. Similarly, this collection is based on a framework of rules. The poems follow the traditionalists by observing the season cycle. Season words, or *kigo*, and season topics, known as *kidai*, are the guideposts that mark the trail. Each poem has seventeen syllables in lines of five, seven, and five syllables. Although not a true representation of the original aesthetic, and by no means necessary to compose outstanding haiku, this form has a balance and grace suitable to the rhythm of English, while also providing a challenge when attempting to distill the essence of a moment into haiku.

The Daily Haiku Reader walks us down a path of awareness through the changing seasons of the year. Each day, a new haiku strikes us with the beauty of nature in the present moment. These brief reflections serve to nourish us, make us mindful, and refresh our inner wellspring. The central act of haiku is capturing the essence of a sensation or event that touches us. The completion of haiku takes place in the reader's mind, where it echoes and awakens, tapping our unique memories and experiences, bridging us to our fellow human beings, and kindling our ancestral connection to the natural world. May these timeless moments find resonance within you.

Matthew Barrington
Autumn 2022
Ithaca

The Daily Haiku Reader

Sun rising over
A new day in the same way
Since the dawn of time

Snowy woodland stream
Outer banks encased in ice
Center swift and mean

Puffed red cardinal
Settles on a longleaf pine
Hiding from the snow

January 4th

Little frozen pond
Thick ice sealing the surface
Slick silver shimmer

Golden sunset rays
Stream across the cloudless sky
Frozen hills aglow

Banks of snow drifting
Slowly moving and shifting
Taken with the wind

Icicles aging
Solidified strong on top
Brittle tapered tip

The doe lifts her head
Pausing to feel the cool breeze
Coat hairs quivering

Winterberry plants
Bring color to frozen lands
Dotted with red fruit

Midnight snow glows blue
Full moon in a cloudless sky
Cold silent glimmer

Black coats standing out
Against the snow at a stream
Two morning minks drink

January 12th

Twigs encased in ice
Rigidly sway in the cold
Frozen cracking sound

Fluttering flurries
Falling in disorganized
Beauty to the ground

Cool air rolls over
Warmer water condensing
Vapor into fog

The black leafless woods
Transformed from darkness to light
Fresh snow glistening

January 16th

Evergreens waving
Back and forth in unison
Bending in billows

Winter rain ceases
As the clouds drifting onward
Continue to pour

January 18th

Frozen waterfall
Ice building up on the rocks
Water still falling

Grey squirrel in the snow
Moving quickly head down low
Pulling up lost nuts

Sun rich clouds and sky
Glowing bright and inviting
Despite deep winter

Martin Luther King Jr. Day

Around the tight bend
A great moose comes thundering
Through tall stacks of snow

Rough lake waters break
Crashing among freezing winds
Shoreline icicles

Flocks of birds across
Open fields covered in snow
Stand against the white

Glowing embers fade
Cooling and crumbling down from
A once crackling fire

Black winter waters
The rushing flow prevents ice
From freezing solid

Hibernating bears
Under a blanket of snow
Tucked warm in their den

Petite cloud alone
In the vast expansive sky
Glowing pink at dusk

Wide river frozen
Under the flow continues
Currents deep unseen

The wind moves across
Freezing lands of ice and snow
Painful bitter blows

Morning snow glistens
On each branch of every tree
Transformed to beauty

Morning light reveals
Tracks and droppings in the snow
Imprints from the night

Rain as cold as ice
Pelting down the fallen snow
Freezing together

The timid groundhog
Munches tender wildflowers
Close by the burrow

Under a pine branch
A locust shell from summer
Dangles in the wind

Temperatures below
Steal the moisture from the snow
Dry and crunching sound

February 5th

Clouds heavy with snow
Looming low on the plateau
Ready for release

At the horizon
Sun rising over water
Orange spreading bright

Unexpected warmth
Brings the woodland creatures out
With false hopes of spring

Black bird on a branch
Bending under the soft weight
Of feathered landings

Puffy fluffy snow
Accumulates on branches
Bending to the earth

Three slender white tails
Standing by the peaceful shore
Suddenly bound off

Morning clouds open
Brightness from the sun bounces
Blinding ice and snow

Sculpted by strong winds
Strong desert rocks arching high
Smooth silent sandstone

Temperature rises
The sound of water dripping
Onto melting snow

Blushing roses bloom
Petals silky soft and rich
In love with the light

St. Valentine's Day

Dozens of small birds
Leap from their perch together
One collective mind

The wind is blowing
Unsettled snow on the ground
Like dry desert sands

Cold air that surrounds
Intensifies in its chill
When the soft wind blows

Grey clouds spread over
A bleak snow-fallen expanse
Sunset splits the two

The tops of pine trees
Pointing upward to the sky
Poking at the clouds

Fat flakes from the sky
Clump together as they fall
Fast toward destiny

White as fallen snow
Swans on silver waters swim
Warmly dressed in down

Earth soaks in the rain
Overnight temperature drops
Freezing solid ground

Through millennia
The ancient crater transforms
Becoming a lake

A torrent of snow
Flakes flying in a flurry
Swarming in the storm

A long black feather
Dropped on the snowy white ground
Raven out of sight

Towering tree trunks
Grown stout and wide slowly push
Great stones in the earth

Fluffy flakes floating
Barely pulled by gravity
Inching toward the ground

Goats of the mountain
Hooves traverse vertical cliffs
Graceful steps and leaps

Grass under the snow
Pressed down and flat on the ground
Pale green without sun

The short-tailed weasel
Black eyes stand out from the snow
Blinking in the cold

Morning light shining
Touching trees and passing through
Shadowing cold ground

An island of snow
Remains after the melting
Of yesterday's storm

Flying high upward
The bold breasted bird perches
And cries her best song

Overnight snow clouds
Leave a trace of their passing
Sparkles in the dawn

Oval openings
Nestle hungry infant birds
Mouths wide to the world

Faded winter lands
Pigments worn away with time
Waiting for the sun

Blue bird on white snow
Wings stretched wide for an instant
Then fluttering fast

Body motionless
Crayfish preying in the stream
Antenna twitching

Temperature rises
The sound of water dripping
Onto melting snow

Green pointed tips rise
Early crocus breaking through
The sealed dormant ground

March 13th

Falling rain seeps down
Saturation in the soil
Hillsides slide away

The return of birds
On this desolate icescape
Brings the hope of spring

Down the sloping hill
Draining water drop by drop
Carves a crooked path

Down from the treetops
The small woodland creatures creep
Stirred by melting warmth

Shamrocks multiply
Glimmering green in the field
Rustled by the breeze

Tributaries flow
To the rivers to the sea
Spilling endlessly

March 19th

A sliver of light
Breaking over morning clouds
Brightening the sky

Dumping heavy rain
The first time in many moons
Washing out the sky

Spring songs returning
Florid birds peck in green grass
Sunshine lights the day

Seafoam green waters
Tucked between the rolling hills
Sunshine shimmering

Red salamander
Returning to the water
Where life first began

Water starts to flow
Slowly filling dry creek beds
Soaking dusty ground

After heavy rain
Humid silence broken by
A single song bird

Little squirrel leaping
The soft plushness of tail fur
Weightless in the air

The warmth of the sun
Bursts over the hill and spreads
Life over the field

Hidden natural spring
Bubbling behind boulders
Deep from underground

Chilly new spring nights
Bring critters out from their dens
Bristling with new life

Recent rounds of rain
Rising waters overflow
Brought by creeks and streams

Towering palm leaves
Catch powerful waves of wind
Bending with the blow

Morning light reveals
The last snow of the season
Green grass poking through

Majestic black bears
Hungry from hibernation
Stretch and sniff the air

Countless drops rain down
Pulling with them particles
Washing out the sky

Heavy soggy logs
Sit inside the flooded bog
Soaked wet to the core

Falcon floating high
Overlooking glacial lakes
Clear water clear sky

April 6th

Wet grass in morning
Shimmering in new daylight
Cold transient dew

Bumblebee tipsy
From nectar of spring flowers
Buzzes side to side

Across the ravine
A fallen tree mossy green
Wet after the rain

Dead dirt on the ground
Making up the earthen base
From which new life flows

Morning's golden glow
Enveloping everything
With its growing warmth

Far rolling terrain
Hills fold into each other
Off in the distance

Long after the fall
The root system harbors life
Sprouting hopeful sprigs

Low lying meadow
Gathers seeping muddy water
Reflecting stillness

Golden breasted bird
Soaring high with outstretched wings
Locked in rigid place

Trees in mild weather
Pushing their leaves through the buds
Unexpected freeze

Egg sack on her back
The spider walks tenderly
Caring for her young

Tall blade of grass
New growth lightly colored green
Bending in the breeze

April 18th

Showers clear away
Leaving still leaves drenched with rain
Wind shakes new drops free

Opossum carries
Six little ones on her back
Waddling away

Poison sumac grows
Around the trunk of a tree
Climbing toward the light

Mud river rushes
Churning up the unseen deep
Drowning bedrock banks

The roots find a way
Slipping inside the slimmest
Cracks along the rocks

Butterfly flutters
Delicately floating high
Weightless in the wings

Rain to stream to creek
Meets the pond through the channel
To the lake and sea

Day's brightness returns
Awash with vivid colors
Still wet with the rain

Succulent aloe
Rejuvenating center
New sprigs reaching up

Saturated slopes
Sans vegetation to hold
Wet mud from sliding

Fresh green tufts of grass
The grazing horses nibble
Strong thick necks bowed down

Just a bumblebee
Visiting all the blossoms
On an apple tree

Swans strongly striding
Looking after downy young
Ripples in the pond

Darling buds of May
Every new appearing sphere
Incubating life

In the faded reeds
A mound made by the beaver
Grows with each new branch

Small delicate leaves
Bend under the tiny weight
Of drizzling rain

Morning light growing
The nightly silence ceases
As sounds fill the air

In the burning sun
Eagle perched on a cactus
Devouring a snake

Cinco de Mayo

Feline in the field
Crouched down and ready to pounce
Silently stalking

New dew dusted dawn
Tall meadow grass shimmering
In the growing light

Fox out on the hunt
Finds shelter from evening rain
Among the dry grove

Lining the long brook
A wild blackberry bramble
Tiny treats sour sweet

Mother and her child
Sleeping soundly side by side
Eyes closed to the world

Every single one
Panicles of white flowers
Bending toward the sun

May 12th

Gently swaying high
Green leaves against a white sky
Backlight silhouette

Hard spiky needles
Old growth cactus menacing
Bright petals in bloom

The great fallen tree
Brings light to the forest floor
Soaked up by saplings

Grasshopper twilight
Springing from a bending weed
Lost in the darkness

Sweet honeysuckle
White petals opening wide
Stamen in the breeze

In the darkened cave
Crystals grow out of the rock
Sparkling in light

The young hemlock tree
Sags under the weight of rain
Clinging to needles

Turkey vulture picks
At the innards of a skunk
And her unborn kits

Wisps of upslope fog
Rise weightlessly and conceal
Branches thick with leaves

The peace of the night
Fallen over bustling lands
The restless find rest

Eggs of infants hatch
Awakening to this world
Blinking to being

Grapevines reaching high
Waving at the shining sun
With a new sprig sprung

The dandelion
Presents its milky seedlings
Waiting for the wind

Vibrant verdant day
Life is teeming everywhere
Old ones pass away

On mountain laurel
Flowers overcrowd the leaves
Blooming profusely

Hummingbird feathers
Defy mighty gravity
Hovering in place

Draping great branches
Spanish moss delicately
Swaying in the breeze

Orange moon rising
Large and full just hovering
At the horizon

Ocean waves crashing
Water rumbles and splashes
Cool mist in the air

Alive in the sun
Birds in the sycamore tree
Singing every one

Evening cool and still
Sweet lavender fills the air
Floating from the fields

Orange tree blossoms
Grow smaller as the center
Swells into sweet fruit

Shining eyes at night
Head of black and tail of white
Lumbering away

Topside fallen down
Great tree toppled to the ground
Roots exposed to sun

The blue-eyed grass blooms
Little tiny lilies lie
Thousands in the sun

Relentless plains wind
Pushing forever forward
Grasses bend over

The songs of seagulls
Held between the roaring sea
And the rocky bluff

Vegetation clings
Hanging on the steepest side
Hugging high hillsides

Soft rain from the day
Clinging droplets bending down
Raspberry branches

Thicket of bamboo
Climbing upward to the sky
Swishing with the wind

June 11th

Shiny black beetle
Revealing a pair of wings
Lifts off into flight

Reeds in the shallows
Swaying with the stillness of
The evening waters

June 13th

Crowding buttercups
Bright and shining beautiful
Golden yellow sheen

Soaking up the sun
Cold-blooded creatures
Stretched out on the rocks

Floating on the air
Being swept from here to there
Dandelion seeds

Stars slowly surface
Making the wide sky sparkle
Rippling with light

Mangroves grip the shore
Tangled roots bring life above
The shallow waters

Post pollination
Yellow flowers on the vine
Transform into fruit

Stones in the forest
Smooth and round among the trees
Green moss coverings

Soft song of summer
Soothing warmth and gentle breeze
Settles in to stay

June 21st

Startled garter snake
Tenses quickly and retreats
Hiding under shade

Tall tree just fallen
Weakened by inward decay
Pale grubs on the ground

June 23rd

Jade basks in the sun
Thick and succulent foliage
Hang on stout branches

Waterfall falling
Splashing rough rocky ledges
White all the way down

The bird lands quickly
Pecking a worm from the ground
Then darts off in flight

Bright whiteness softly
Brimming in the open boll
Cotton in the sun

Flower past its time
Petals rough and rigid dry
Drooping toward the ground

Under every tree
The flowering trillium
Brings light to the shade

Relaxing waters
Warmed by unencumbered rays
Striking the shallows

Branches softly sway
Wind in the weeping willow
Ripples like water

Rabbit running scared
Hind legs firing rapidly
Lost in thick brambles

Nightly encounter
A chorus of cicadas
Resonate their songs

Fish diving deep down
Down to unthinkable depths
Hidden from the light

Radiant beams glow
The light unencumbered shines
Illuminating

Independence Day

Lemons on the tree
Swell and ripen in the sun
Dropping one by one

Calming reflection
The seemingly still water
Is not still at all

Particles surround
Dust floating still in the air
Illuminated

Heavy flies swarming
Encircling a fallen
Carcass in the woods

Sweet scent of summer
Flower pollen in the air
Softly lingering

Mushrooms are rising
Quickly and delicately
Out of the decay

Sandpiper piping
Darting and zipping along
Where sand sinks to sea

Closed in nightly dark
Succulent flowers spread wide
Open at first light

July 13th

Dusty bull standing
Motionless in the burning sun
Tail swatting a fly

Jasmine flowering
Lingering with the breezes
From fields far away

July 15th

Seagulls close to shore
Open beaks and piercing shrieks
Circling the sky

In a husk of burr
The chestnut tree bears its fruit
Nuts hidden inside

Tiny smudge of light
Andromeda galaxy
Hangs between the stars

Uncountable calls
Come from nocturnal insects
Innumerable

Rocky mountain ridge
Packed with dense hard frozen snow
Summer never shows

Waves break at daybreak
Fresh morning foam is frothing
Washing up on shore

The sun at its peak
Fiercely hot and sweltering
Timid flowers droop

Ground and grass lay wet
Heavy air filled with moisture
Stormy remnants

July 23rd

Endless plains under
Far and high wide open skies
Vast eternity

Tail in the water
Quickly back and forth swimming
Lost among the weeds

Life comes to a close
Quickly for the low insect
Accidentally

Reflective waters
Casting crystal images
From the distant shore

Petals opening
Spreading wider through the day
Imperceptibly

The sweltering heat
Drying moisture from the earth
Turning dirt to dust

Delicate fern leaves
Shaded in the summer breeze
Nodding lazily

Downy weightlessness
Feather flutters to the ground
Origins unknown

Gator in the sun
Eyes at ease and mouth smiling
Breathing happily

Ripping at the sands
The strong undertow draws back
Everything it can

A withering stump
Dried in the parching heat
Insects chip away

The light vanishes
From the stars in the night sky
As dawn approaches

The Joshua tree
Takes strong root in arid sands
Determination

Plants without the rain
Turn stiff and deathly brittle
Life has left the roots

Waving in the wind
The spider's web blowing free
Silently flapping

Touching emptiness
The mountains become desert
Vast endless flatness

Warm radiant rays
Shine through unencumbered skies
With blinding brightness

Air heavy with salt
Deposits flaky crystals
On surrounding rocks

August 10th

Thrashing in a storm
Branches whip and bend backward
Helpless in the wind

Fruit flies multiply
Swarming together in flight
Moving senselessly

Tumbleweeds rolling
Ushered by the endless wind
No destination

In clear cool water
A school of fish by the rocks
Huddles from the waves

August 14th

Arid desert floor
Cracked clay baking in the heat
Vegetation gone

Moist wetness surrounds
A shady patch of mushrooms
Life from withered logs

Angelic waters
Hold the highest clarity
All below is seen

Strong gusts of wind push
The turkey vulture upward
Effortlessly high

Atmospheric hue
Alive on distant mountains
Painting them in blue

Stream over bedrock
Swelling from overnight rain
Rushing down below

Spotted owl perching
Body still but head turning
All the way around

Fires raging bright
Embers lifted by strong winds
Ignite new timber

One single drop drips
And splatters a small pattern
On dry dusty ground

Forest of hemlocks
Treetops inching toward the sky
Ever reaching high

Across open skies
A single leaf in the wind
Not a tree in sight

Water's reflection
Forever rearranging
Lazy wavy light

Old leaves withering
New ones uncurling with life
Eternal cycle

Slow drips of water
Each absorbed into the ground
Barely any sound

Strong saltwater wind
Rushes inland from the sea
Brisk and forcefully

Sunlit canyon walls
Echoing the cries of birds
Flying between them

Trickling water
Flows into rushing torrents
After a downpour

Precision in flight
Birds glide just above the pond
Hanging between worlds

September 1st

Growing tall in droves
Goldenrod in heavy sun
Turns pastures vibrant

Full moon on birch trees
Wrapping around the white bark
Glowing brilliant blue

Great cavern cascade
Thundering in the chasm
Only water's roar

Distant thunderstorm
Darkness falling between clouds
And the horizon

September 5th

Shaking in the straw
The meadow mouse darts away
Rapid heart beating

Shadows from the moon
Sharply cast on the bottom
Waters calm and clear

Tail up to the sky
Red squirrel works to uncover
A hidden bounty

After days of storms
The clouds run out of raindrops
The first bird returns

September 9th

Whole bunches of grapes
Dropping under their own weight
Lay beneath the vine

Midnight mist nestles
The base of the foothill range
Covering palm leaves

September 11th

Sharp flash in the sky
Bright lightning bolts to the ground
Tall trees topple down

9/11 Remembrance Day

Glowing through the trees
The sun a perfect circle
Warms the horizon

Fallen leaf circles
In an eddy in a stream
Caught with the current

A snail on a stone
Inching along with its shell
Shiny streak behind

New dew dusted dawn
Awakens slumbering fawns
Tracks across wet grass

Pollen in the air
Suspended in tranquil flight
Let loose from the trees

September 17th

Hundreds of bird calls
Suddenly drop to silence
Scared from a sharp sound

Steady whistling wind
Passing over a dead tree
Just right to form sound

Dead animal drowned
Floating on the bank current
Tail weightless waving

Fresh moist sandy soil
Pulling up the stock and roots
Critters excavate

September 21st

New evening's chill makes
Vapors from the warm water
Rise as mist anew

Fallen from the flock
Wings will never feel the air
Broken on the ground

Half moon on the rise
Hanging low in empty skies
Severed perfectly

Powerful winds push
Clouds high in the sky along
No breeze on the ground

Early morning frost
Sparkling in the same sun
That will destroy it

Streams dump in the creek
Rushing torrents rage and rise
Cacophonous roar

September 27th

Formless bright white sky
Fading into arching trees
Woven with the fog

Warmth from the water
Encounters cold air above
Sea smoke drifting in

The sounds of high wind
Rattling rushing raging raw
Blasting forcefully

Shadows from the sun
Bright day followed by bright night
Shadows from the moon

Crisp cold morning air
Hangs silently in stillness
Condensating breaths

Cool water trickles
Slowly down a steep shale cliff
Darkening the stone

October 3rd

Some will grow to trees
Tiny brown cones on the ground
Future tamaracks

Rising to the night
Steam lifts off the warm waters
Slow to dissipate

Thinning of branches
One by one leaves blow away
Lightly tumble down

In depthless waters
The sea serpents hide their home
Cold and lightless deep

Wind precedes a storm
Whitecaps atop the water
Churning and choppy

Hot and heavy heat
The sun beats down from above
In autumnal days

Freshly fallen leaves
Golden yellow and orange
Hide the rough dirt ground

Creeping silently
The fog over the water
Conceals everything

Thin translucent leaves
Catch beams from the setting sun
Colors bursting bright

After the harvest
Empty fields covered with frost
In the morning chill

October 13th

New leaves on the ground
Turning from a bright yellow
To dark brittle brown

Horses with heads down
In the cold foggy morning
Grazing frosted grass

Colorful maple
Holding on to foliage
Before the great fall

The wind and the waves
Have taken the sands back home
Far out to the sea

Hail falls and bounces
Settling still in the grass
Thousands of small pearls

Late night wind rages
Thrashing branches back and forth
Dying leaves take flight

A large pine cone drops
Bouncing into the ravine
Lost to the great depth

Wounded in the hunt
The beating heart strains to pump
Blood that should be there

Floating falling leaves
Hanging in between two worlds
Lightly drifting down

Mist among mountains
Cloaking trees in the morning
Still wispy whiteness

October 23rd

Barren and exposed
Leafless trees against the dawn
Branches stark and black

Pumpkins in the patch
Orange orbs poking above
Wide leaves and the vine

Pine needles falling
Delicate and golden brown
Landing silently

Colorful pin oak
Left side filled with vibrant leaves
Other side naked

The last of darkness
Shadows from the rising sun
Vanish into day

Snow on autumn trees
The quick passage of seasons
Starts with the first snow

Tree stumps charred and black
After the inferno passed
Jut out from the ground

Blown straight off the bough
A single gust strips fall leaves
Coloring the ground

Silked in symmetry
Spider centered in a web
Motionless waiting

Grey skies losing light
Midday as the sun goes down
Early darkening

Red orange yellow
Every golden shade of these
Covering the trees

Thunder shakes the ground
Lightning flashes night to day
Heavy rain pours down

November 4th

An old apple tree
Overripe fruit drops below
Rotting on the ground

Dry leaves rustling
Turning over on the ground
Hollow scraping sound

November 6th

Raindrops on treetops
Pitter patter splattering
All the long way down

Snow on autumn leaves
Turning white bark and branches
Quickly melts away

November 8th

Scattered leaves crumble
Veins empty and drained of life
Brittle broken form

Forest reaching tall
Treetops swirling in circles
Creaking in the wind

November 10th

Frigid drops of rain
Hit the ground as solid ice
Hardened by harsh winds

Tremendous oak trees
Towering mightily high
Touching lofty climes

Veteran's Day

Breezes send dead leaves
Somersaulting in circles
Skipping with new life

Great elevation
The rocky ridges below
All covered in clouds

Suddenly snowing
Thick fluffy flakes fill the sky
Coming from nowhere

Leaves spiral in flight
Twisting and drifting straight up
Circling back down

November 16th

Wood smoke in the wind
Being blown from a distant
Fire in the woods

November 17th

Snow on the hillside
Through the thousand leafless trees
Blanketing steep earth

Long clouds turning pink
But for only a moment
Within seconds gone

Huddled together
Ducks in the snowy water
Bobbing up and down

Whipping whistling wind
Relentless and frigid cold
Knows no obstacle

Leaves soaked with water
Swept into murky puddles
Turning into mud

Morning snow melted
Disappearing unnoticed
Leaving empty ground

Rising mountainside
Colors faded and fallen
Evergreens shine through

New ice on the pond
Shining in the morning sun
Frozen overnight

Blackened clouds crowding
Lilac purple sunset skies
Fast fading dark hues

Turkey foraging
Head down pecking tail up high
Feathers to the sky

Treetops now empty
Every leaf has fallen down
Blanketing the ground

Icy pelts of rain
Riding on the gusting gales
Crashing to the ground

As foliage grows scarce
Mother's young try suckling milk
From dry barren teats

Forest floor all calm
Treetops caught by strong winds wave
Fallen leaves lay still

Along the shoreline
Ice begins to form and creeps
Out into the deep

December 2nd

Snowflakes disappear
Vanishing at first light touch
Meeting solid ground

Uncurling pink blooms
The drooping cactus flowers
Amidst the cold chill

December 4th

Wet snow attaches
Only to the side of trees
Brunting the harsh wind

Branches without leaves
Stand motionless at midnight
Absolute stillness

Moving with the wind
Thin grey clouds accumulate
Makers of snowflakes

Mystical colors
The enchanting aurora
Lights up the night sky

Pearl Harbor Day

The last of the leaves
Hang on in the bitter wind
Withered and flapping

The sun breaking through
Behind an afternoon rain
Ignites bright the sky

Snow on the plateau
Piles up before it comes
To the lands below

White ashen blanket
Hiding hot sleeping embers
Strike fast into flames

Several year sapling
Bends under the weight of snow
Tip touching the ground

Meteor showers
Etch brief pathways in dark skies
A long journey's end

The grey skies above
Scatter and dim vibrant light
From the hidden sun

Branches brown and bare
Powdered from the trunk to top
Glowing in whiteness

The sounds from high winds
Keep rattling rushing raging
Howling forcefully

Exposed in winter
Nest atop a barren tree
Warms a family

A dusting of snow
Touches all the tops of things
Shimmering in white

Simple slender twigs
Support freshly fallen snow
Flakes piling up high

Silent morning sky
The same whiteness as the snow
Brightness envelops

A wall of winter
White from the ground to the sky
Millions of flakes fly

December 22nd

High above the clouds
The sun still shines brilliantly
Whether the weather

Great waters recede
Leaving sandy banks exposed
Grains swept by cold winds

December 24th

Puffy fluffy flakes
Inching their way to the ground
As slow as can be

Noses in the cold
Reindeer in the great white north
Wander through the snow

Darkness vast and clear
Stunning silence of the sky
Outer space drawn near

A rare desert snow
Saguaro cactus turned white
Needles cradle flakes

December 28th

Winter wind and rain
Cut down dried and withered weeds
Breaking brittle stems

High on the mountain
Snowflakes slowly upward drift
Climbing to the sky

The day almost done
Fox running cold in the dusk
Body disappears

Sun setting over
All the days that came before
Just to rise once more

New Year's Eve

Made in the USA
Middletown, DE
06 November 2023